How Pennie Got Her Groove Back

By:

Penelope "Pennie" Taylor

How Pennie Got Her Groove Back

By

Penelope "Pennie" Taylor

Published By:

ABM Publications
A division of Andrew Bills Ministries Inc.
PO Box 6811, Orange, CA 92863

www.abmpublications.com

ISBN: 978-1-931820-60-8

DEDICATION

This book is dedicated to my Lord and Savior Jesus Christ who always seems to amaze me. I thought He would allow me to write just one book, but He let me know there is more to me than this.

To all my spiritual sisters who feel like you have lost your groove for Jesus. He longs to come to your rescue. The devil does not want us to get our spiritual groove back because he knows that with our spiritual grove we are armed and extremely dangerous with the word of God.

Be Blessed in the Lord,

Minister Pennie Taylor

TABLE OF CONTENTS

PENELOPE "PENNIE" TAYLOR

ACKNOWLEDGEMENTS

I would like to thank my Pastors, Pastor Billy and Minister LaWanda Taylor and the Walking by Faith Church Family, whom I love dearly. Thanks for being the church family that you are, so loving and caring of others.

To Women of Destiny, You know who you are. Thank you for being my confidant, you are always there whenever I need you.

To the readers of this book, thank you for making the investment, both in my efforts and, on a greater scale, trusting God to give you back your spiritual groove.

In memory of my deceased mother Gracie Blackshear, thank you for shaping me into the woman that I am today. You have done an awesome job. In memory of my deceased father James Sires, I thank God I found you before it was too late.

To my Facebook Ministry, God is taking this ministry to another dimension.

To my family and friends, thank you for putting up with me. You have blessed me more than you will ever know. To my husband Burnar, my soul mate. Thank you for always being there for me. When I said I couldn't you said I could.

I love you all,
Minister Pennie Taylor

1

PENELOPE "PENNIE" TAYLOR

Chapter 1

HOW I GOT MY GROOVE BACK

Some of you may be thinking, I can't wait to see how Pennie got her groove back. Keep on reading, because the best is yet to come. I know some of you are in a dry spot in your life right now. The idea that you are reading this book lets me know that you are interested in getting your groove back. Throughout this book I will be talking about how I got my groove back. (Talking about my spiritual groove). I was in a dry spot just like some of you are right now. I felt so empty inside because I knew God had more for me to do. The only way to know what God has for you to do is to seek his face. We need to always depend on God and God alone.

Ephesians 1:4-5
4. According as he hath chosen us in him before the foundation of the world, that we should be holy and without blame before him in love:
[5.] Having predestinated us unto the adoption of children by Jesus Christ to himself, according to the good pleasure of his will.

Can I share a secret with you? Your worth and you purpose do not depend on what others think of you, or what you have done in life. Your worth and purpose depends on God and God alone. If you place your hand in God's hand He will give you your spiritual groove back. That's how I got my groove back. I want you to know that nothing in life happens by chance. God always has a plan whether we like

His plan or not. Even when we go through trials and tribulations, God still has a plan for our life. Everything that you are going through, all that you are dealing with has one ultimate purpose, that you may know the love of God and live in the light of His perfect love for you.

When you feel like you want to throw in the towel, don't do it. That is the trick of the enemy to cause you to abort your destiny. If I would have listened to the enemy, I would have aborted my destiny when I was in the 7th grade. I would have died in the 7th grade. God had already assured my momma that he had a plan for my life. Now that I am 55 years old I am beginning to walk in my destiny. The more we stay in the word of God, the more we will be able to hear his voice. We must learn how to recognize God's voice, and that is through his written word.

Isaiah 30:21
^{21} And thine ears shall hear a word behind thee, saying, this is the way, walk ye in it, when ye turn to the right hand, and when ye turn to the left.

If you want an intimate relationship with God you must consistently and faithfully set aside time so that God can communicate with you through his word and by His Spirit. We've got to walk this thing out. Talk with God when you pray, and listen to Him when He speaks to you. Everything you need to know to have a prosperous life is in the word of God. If you put yourself in a position for God to meet with you, then everything else will fall into perspective. Then you will learn to recognize his voice. I used to have a hard time recognizing God's voice. I used to always ask God to show me a sign. Sometimes he would show me a sign and sometimes he wouldn't. We just have to trust him since he always knows what's best for us. We trust everything else in life. Why not trust God?

Somebody reading this book may feel like you will never get your spiritual groove back, but if God can give me back my groove, He can do the same for you. Those of you that are in a dry spot right now and feel like you don't know where to turn, always know that God is right there to carry you through. Maybe you have lost a loved one, maybe you are having problems in your marriage, or maybe your kids just don't want to do right. I advise you to turn every one of those situations over to the Lord and He will see you through.

Philippians 1:21
[21.] For to me to live is Christ, and to die is gain.

I use to wonder what Paul was saying in this scripture. God gave me a revelation of what this scripture really means. If you live in Christ, when you die you will have joy. Even if you live in Christ while you are alive you can still have joy. That's when we begin to get our spiritual groove back. When we live in Christ, there is always joy if you want to have it.

James 1:2
My brethren, count it all joy when ye fall into divers temptations.

Some of you may be saying. How can I count it all joy when my husband just ran off with my best friend? How can I count it all joy when all my furniture just got repossessed? How can I count it all joy when I just lost my job? Even when we are going through there is still a reason to be joyful, because the situation could always be worst. When God is your focus everything else will fall into place. Stop trying to please people. God is the only one we need to please. He will cause people to be pleased, but if not. OH WELL!

Galatians 1:10
For do I now persuade men, or God? Or do I seek to please men? For if I yet pleased men, I should not be the servant of Christ.

When we are set free from the bondage of trying to please others and trying to please ourselves then no one will make us miserable or dissatisfied. I use to love getting the approval of others, but when I really came to myself, I discovered that the only approval I need is from God.

When God approves you He will open that door for you to walk into whatever it is that He has planned for you. When people are pushing your buttons or getting on your last borrowed nerves, as my friend Sister Mary Jones would always say, it's all for a reason. I didn't know at the time that my buttons were getting pushed, but as I begin to walk into my destiny I realized it was all a part of God's plan for my purpose. He knew the right people to use to push my buttons. He knew the right people to send to hurt me. He knew the right people to send to betray me. When I look back over my life I want to thank God for everybody that He used to help push me into my destiny, whether it was good or bad it was part of God's plan. It all worked for my good. How do I know it worked for my good? Look at what the scripture says.

Romans 8:28

28. And we know that all things work together for good to them that love God, to them who are the called according to his purpose.

This scripture does not apply to everyone. You have to be called according to God's purpose in Christ Jesus. When you are going through hard times if you would meditate on this scripture God will give you peace in the mist of your struggle. I dare you to trust God. When you trust God He will begin to amaze you until it becomes so scary. It doesn't take God long to do anything. We serve the almighty powerful God.

In this hour that we are living in, God is getting ready to blow our mind like never before. Before you can turn around God will have answered your prayers. I want you to know that God is not going to answer your prayers if you are being disobedient to His word. His word comes with stipulations. He says I will do this if you do that. God is not a God that He should lie and He will not go back on His word. I LOVE THE LORD. Why? Because He heard my cry and He came to my rescue. I thank God for giving me my groove back.

Know that God didn't call us to sit down, He called us to serve. God wants to work miracles every day through us. When you are rooted and grounded in God you should be able to get a prayer through. When somebody comes to you in church with a headache you should be able to lay hands on them and they should recover. It's time for people to be healed in the house of the Lord. There are so many people playing church, but it's time to get real with God. The anointing is what breaks the yoke.

One reason we can't do the work God is requiring of us is because we have lost our spiritual grove, we have let so many things keep us distracted until we can't hear what God is speaking to us. If you want to hear from God you need to get in a quiet place and SHUT UP and let God talk. Sometimes we want to do all the talking when God is saying SHUT UP and let me do the talking. I know this from experience. When God tells us to do something we want to know why? Just do like NIKE. Just do it. If God has told you to do something He has already made the way for you to get it done. Ask God to anoint your eyes so you can see what He is trying to show you.

How many times have you asked God to use you, but when He started using you, you become scared. I know this has happen to me many times. I just finally told God He can do the driving; I am going to just sit in the back seat and where ever He takes me is where I am going to go. We need to have faith that God will get us to where we need to be if we would just TRUST Him.

Amos 3:3 Can two walk together, except they be agreed?

I don't want anybody walking with me that is not in agreement with me. If you are praying for one thing and they are praying for something totally different GUESS WHAT? It is not going to work. You have to agree on what you are praying and believing God for. I know that God will answer your prayers if you would seek His face and believe in His word. The devil will do all he can to try and block your blessings. My thing is this, if you let him. The choice is yours. How bad do you want the blessings of God? The devil thinks he is smart, but in all reality he is dumb. He doesn't know that when he messes with a child of God he is only making us stronger and wiser.

I say devil keep elevating me. God has taken my mess and turned it into a message for His people.
My friend Rochelle Mudd said. "Pennie, God will gather your pain together and make a message out of your mess", and that is what He is doing for me right now. I am gathering information that God has given me over the years and compiling them into this book. I tell you this is my second book and God is really putting this thing together. So I say to all my readers, the mess that you are going through with right now will one day be your message. Everything that God allows us to go through with is not for our glory, but for His Glory! Some things that we go through can be for our children, our grandchildren, our spouses, or even our co-workers. God wants to show himself in places where we don't even think he will show up. Everything that God allows to come our way is for a purpose. He uses even the greatest error and the deepest hurt to mold us into a person of worth and value.

I hate seeing God's people walking around all burdened down like they don't have anything to live for. So many people are calling it quits in this last hour because things are getting to tough for them to handle. If this is you stop right now and repeat this prayer.

> Father God, in the name of Jesus. Lord I come with a heavy heart Lord, but I know that you are able to deliver me from anything. Lord you said in Matthew 6:33 if I seek you first you will add everything else that I need. Lord I want to seek your face

like never before. Lord bless me in every
way. Lord let your will be done in my life. In
Jesus name I pray. Amen

After praying this pray, I hope that God will speak to your
spirit in a mighty way. The God that I serve is able to do
more than we ask of Him.

It's time to start laughing in the devils face. The devil
doesn't like when we laugh in his face. He is nothing but a
liar and a deceiver. Tell him you are more than a
conqueror in Christ Jesus. Let him know you are the head
and not the tail. Let him know that no weapon formed
against you or your family shall prosper. When you begin
to tell the devil this and believe it you are on your way to
getting your spiritual groove back.

Chapter 2

BACK AT CHURCH

I was going to church Sunday after Sunday, Wednesday after Wednesday and was still feeling empty inside. I felt like I was losing my spiritual groove. I kept asking God why I was feeling this way.

I use to hear people say that the church is supposed to be like a hospital, the place where you go to get spiritual advice, the place where you go to receive your breakthrough, the place where you go to receive healing and to get relief, but I was going to church and was not getting anything. I know some of you may be feeling what I am talking about. I came to realized that my Pastor had carried me as far as he could carry me. I had been in that place for 53 years. I was comfortable there. No hard feelings to my former Pastor, but I came to realize it was time for me to move on.

Sometimes we try to stay in a place of complacency, when in reality God has told us it's time to move. When we go to school we don't stay in the first grade for five years. We don't even stay in the twelfth grade for five years. So what makes us think we can stay in one spot with God for five years? God is a God of promotions. With God comes promotions and elevation. I could have stayed in the same spot and became bitter and angry because God was not answering my prayers fast enough, or the way I wanted Him to. I promise if you do things God's way he will make everything alright.

God did not create us to be robots. He created us with the choice to move forward or get left behind. The choice is ours. I felt like my life was becoming stale. But when I obeyed God and decided to do things His way and not mine I begin to get my spiritual groove back. God says in His word we can have what we ask as long as it's in His will. I fought and fought with the decision I was about to face, but in reality my time at my old church was up. No matter how hard I tried to fight it I had to leave. God let me know there were too many women attached to me that I needed to help get delivered. I was keeping other women from reaching their destiny because I would not move when God told me to move.

A prophetess told me about 3 years ago that my Pastor had carried me as far as he could carry me. I didn't know what she was talking about. I asked the Lord what she was talking about. How can you outgrow a Pastor? I found out that you could outgrow a Pastor. My spirit man was craving for more than I was getting from where I was. God was also trying to move my husband. After we listened to God we decided to make that decision as a family and move on.

We have been at our new church since June of 2013. I tell you my spirit man is growing like never before. If you are in a place and you know you are not growing in the Lord it might be time for you to seek God like never before and see what he has to say about the situation. I am learning never to move without consulting the Lord. He knows our beginning to our end. We need to stop listening to people that want you to leave a place because they have left.

When God tells you to move and you refuse He will make your stay very miserable. That's what the Lord did for me.

We must remember that this Christian journey is not about pleasing people, it's about pleasing almighty God. I thank God for my new Pastor and First Lady, Pastor Billy and Minister LaWanda Taylor. My family and I are learning a lot under their leadership. It's good to have Godly leaders in this day and time that are really watching for your soul as the bible says. I had a hard time understanding the scripture that says obey them that have the rule over you. Let me post it so you can study it for yourself.

Hebrews 13:17 [17] Obey them that have the rule over you, and submit yourselves: for they watch for your souls, as they that must give account, that they may do it with joy, and not with grief: for that is unprofitable for you.

It takes a Godly leader to watch for your soul, not wolves in sheep clothing because the bible tells us to watch out for them. This scripture is talking about submitting to Godly leaders, someone that has your best interest at heart and not an agenda or a motive. Someone who is led by the spirit and not by their flesh. So many leaders have taken this scripture out of context to fit their own agenda. Churches these days are becoming like a cult. You do as I say no matter what God says.

God is raising up women and men in this hour to carry out the mandate for His kingdom. Women have been put down by leaders thinking they are not supposed to speak in church. I say the devil is a lie. Who were the first to appear at the tomb? Women, if we continue to believe the lies of men we as women will never fulfill our destiny that God has laid out for us. God has wonderful things in store for his women just as he does for his men. God has no respecter person. In God there is neither male nor female. Watch this.

Galatians 3:28 There is neither Jew nor Greek, there is neither bond nor free, there is neither male nor female: for ye are all one in Christ Jesus.

What does this scripture mean? It means that God can use women just like He can use a man. If women all over the world would stay home from church one week and let the men handle everything, what kind of churches would there be. Women play the key role in churches today. And God made sure of that. Man cannot stop what God has ordained.

It's time for leaders to line up with God and put away that prideful spirit. There are seven things in scripture that God hates.

Proverbs chapter 6:16-21
¹⁶ These six things doth the LORD hate: yea, seven are an abomination unto him:
¹⁷ A proud look, a lying tongue, and hands that shed innocent blood,
¹⁸ A heart that deviseth wicked imaginations, feet that be swift in running to mischief,
¹⁹ A false witness that speaketh lies, and he that soweth discord among brethren.
²⁰ My son, keep thy father's commandment, and forsake not the law of thy mother:
²¹ Bind them continually upon thine heart, and tie them

about thy neck

If the Lord hates these things we as Christians should hate them as well. We all need to take these scriptures and apply them to our life every day. God wants us to obey his word so we will eat the good of the land.

Isaiah 1:19If you are willing and obedient, you shall eat the good of the land.

Who wouldn't want to eat the good of the Land? God has given us so many promises in his word if we would obey them. There are blessings when we obey the Lord, and there are also curses when we disobey the Lord. I am learning every day and asking God to teach me how to be obedient to His word.

There is no one like our God. When your midnight hours turn into daylight God is still there to comfort you. In times of sorrow you can always call on the Lord. We try to call on everybody but the Lord and they can't help us. God makes it that way so that we will learn how to call on him as our first result and not our last. No matter what goes on in our lives, we have strength through the spirit of God. God has promised to take care of all our needs.

Ephesians 3:20 says Now unto him that is able to do exceeding abundantly above all that we ask or think, according to the power that worketh in us.

If the Lord put you in a situation, He knows how to bring you out. You need to be glad you went to jail. You need to be glad your momma whipped your behind. You need to glad you spent them 18 years in prison. You need to be glad you got caught. You need to be glad God snatched you up out of the world. If God brought you to it, He will bring you through it. Be encouraged in the Lord.

Chapter 3

ARMED AND EXTREMELY DANGEROUS

I have had the opportunity to minister to women all over the world, whether in person, on the phone, or through my Facebook ministry. God has opened that door and there are women out there that are hurting. Jesus came to give us an abundant life. He does not want us walking around with our heads hanging down. But Guess What? The devil does. Anytime the devil thinks he sees a way to enter into your life that is what he will do. Give no space for the devil to enter in. I thank God for the opportunity to be able to reach and minister to hurting women. If God's women can come together and get on one accord the devil knows we are dangerous creatures in God.

How many of you are waiting to give birth to your ministry? This is the season that God is bringing forth those who are in labor and ready to give birth. All you have to do is P.U.S.H. Pray Until Something Happens.

On April 20th 2013 I gave birth to WOMEN OF DESTINY. God allowed me to have my first women's conference. I said in my first book that God was birthing a Ministry out of me called Women of Destiny. When God is birthing something out of you it will not be easy. Just like having a baby you will have to go through the hurt, the pain, the agony, the discomfort, but when the baby comes forth it is a beautiful feeling. I had three children so I know the beauty that comes from child birth. I thank God for my birthing process, because the Ministry He has entrusted me with will bring healing, and deliverance to hurting women all over the world.

Women that have never been in church were at that conference. Women with alcohol on their breath were at that conference. Women that were crushed to pieces were at that conference. When they left, they didn't leave the same way they came. They came expecting something from God and God was right there to meet them at their point of needs. I thank God for believing in me and using me as one of His chosen vessels for this assignment that He has set before me.

Sisters, are you your Sister's keeper? Brothers, are you your Brother's keeper? We need to keep each other accountable. God never told us to walk this road alone.

When we are armed with the word of God we are extremely dangerous, and the devil doesn't like it. We must wear the word at all times. The devil will try to sneak up on you when you least expect it. That's why you've got to hide the word in your heart so that you will not sin against God.

There will be times in your life when a situation comes up and you can't run and get your bible. There will be times in your life when you are driving down the highway and you need that word. You can't say, "Hold on devil I've got to go back home and get my bible." NO YOU CAN'T. That's why it's important to know the word. The devil is not playing in this hour. He is really roaming around seeking whom he can defile. The world does not want to see you achieve, but God does. You can rise above your situation. You can rise above the odds that you think are against you.

The only way you can reach your destiny is to seek God and let him drive you there. I told my husband I didn't know where God was taking us, but we were going to sit in the back seat and let Him do the driving. When you let God do the driving He will get you where you need to go on time. God want us to reach our destiny. He is not going to force us to get there, but He will cause oppositions if we get out of line with His will for our life. Elder Steven Fluker told me I was going to have to be strong in this next round. He told me that everything I will ever need in life was locked up in my purpose. He said my Joy was in my purpose. My peace was in my purpose. My love was in my purpose.

I was took that Rhema word and I begin to apply it to my life. I am now pursuing my purpose. After I knew my purpose then I was able to fulfill my destiny. Stop looking for a dead end situation. Keep pressing on! I know it's hard to keep pressing on when you're fifteen year old comes and tells you she's pregnant.

I know it's hard when the judge tells you your son just got 25 years in prison for armed robbery, but even in the mist of the pressing on we know that we still have a purpose in this life. The enemy job is to get us distracted and off track, but the God I serve is still able to bring us out just like his word says. Where there is movement there is life. My church, Walking by Faith, is on the move for Christ. I thank God for my Pastor and First Lady, Pastor Billy and Minister LaWanda Taylor. Love you guys.

There are so many clowns and monkeys in church trying to play with God. God knows who you are. His Holy place is not a circus as some may seem to think it is. We've got men standing before God's people doing praise and worship with skinny jeans on. They are so tight you can't even bend over. You've got ladies coming in church and walking right up to the front and trust to sit on the front row with your legs wide open. What happened to the mothers that use to put the towel across our lap?

God forbid you try to say anything to them. What do they do? Run and tell the Pastor. The Pastor should be the first one to say something about the way things are going on in God's holy place. Nowadays the preachers are too busy themselves entertaining the wrong spirit and you wonder why your church don't have any anointing. Everything in God's house starts with the head. If the head is cut off then the body can't live. When are we going to get back to the things of God? I know God is very angry with His people for allowing so much chaos to happen around us.

God is calling us back to holiness. One reason we can't get our spiritual groove back is because we are too busy trying to act and do things like the world does them. Once we come on the Lord's side we are in the world, but not of the world, meaning God has set us aside for His Glory. If we say God has delivered us from a lot of things, then we should show some signs that we have been delivered. God don't expect for us to change all at once, but we should be striving every day for perfection.

We will never be perfect in this life, but we need to become better than we were the day before. People should see your fruit (the way you live) and what you say. When people look at you they can say, I want some of that. God wants us to acknowledge the fruit of the spirit in our life.

Galatians 5:22-23

[22] But the fruit of the Spirit is love, joy, peace, longsuffering, gentleness, goodness, faith,

[23] Meekness, temperance: against such there is no law.

If you are not processing these fruits pray and ask God to help you. Nothing comes easy, but if you seek God I promise He will help you. I am still working on some of these qualities in my life because one thing about it is that I have not arrived yet. I still have a long way to go in this Christian walk. I can truly say that growth comes with time. You must have a desire to want to grow. It's time to get off milk and take off the pull-ups. I am wearing my big girl panties now. I thank God he allowed me to take off the pull-ups. God is bringing His women together for such a time as this, because with God's word on the inside of us we are armed and extremely dangerous.

PENELOPE "PENNIE" TAYLOR

CHAPTER 4

DON'T FAKE IT!

I have heard a lot of people say Fake it till you make it. I say baby, you better take that mask off. THE ACT IS OVER. Jesus came to set you FREE. If people can't accept you for who God called you to be you need to LET THEM GO! Why would God want you to fake it? He wants us to be real with who we are. That's a lot of our problem; we don't want to get real with ourselves. We are too busy worrying about what somebody thinks about us till we have forgotten how to be real. Every time somebody opens their mouth they say. Thank you Jesus, Praise the Lord, and time they get from around you they are cursing God with their lips. God says this should not be. Blessings and cursing should not come out the same mouth.

James 3:10 [10] Out of the same mouth proceedeth blessing and cursing. My brethren, these things ought not so to be. These are not my words, but the words of the Lord. How do you think God feels when this kind of stuff comes out of His children mouth? We should bless the Lord at all times and let his praise continually be in our mouth. (Psalms 34:1) We bless God by doing what pleases Him.

Whenever God gives me a word for his people I want there to be change in their life. We shouldn't go to church and leave the same way we came. When God shows up in the sanctuary things should change. I don't believe you can get in the presence of God and remain the same. Being in God's presences should make a difference in your life. So whatever you need God to do in your life I believe He will do it just for the asking. God wants to bless us like never before. We need to position ourselves to receive His blessings. Stop getting jealous when God blesses your sister or brother. The same thing He did for somebody else He will do for you. But how bad do you want it?

John 14:14 If ye shall ask any thing in my name, I will do it
I use to think if I asked God for a million dollars I would get it. If I asked God for a 5 bedroom mansion I would get it. Yes, God can give us those things, but are they in His will? Why would God give us those things and He already knows we don't have a job to keep up the mortgage. Why would He give us a million dollars when we want give a person twenty dollars. We are going broke trying to keep up with the Jones. I came to the conclusion that the Jones had to file bankruptcy. I did a women conference called TAKE OFF THE MASK. I want you to know; there were women there that were broken for real. When are you going to get to a point where it doesn't matter what people are saying about you as long as you get to Jesus? When we get that mindset and attitude we will be unstoppable in the things of God.

God is not playing in these last and evil days. He is getting ready to tear down some playhouses and scatter some toys. He is also getting ready to tear down some strongholds that have had you bound for the last seven years. Know that God's perfect number is seven. God has been dealing with me on the numbers three, seven, and eight.

The very thing that is causing you not to get closer to God He is getting ready to strip it from up under you. I don't know who this word is for but God does. If this word is for you, you need to give God some praise right where you are. It's time to get your groove back. Even in the mist of your struggler, your tears, and your pain God has a blessing with your name on it. Reach up and grab it. Deliverance comes from God. I thank God for delivering me out of the hands of the enemy. Count it all Joy even when things don't always go the way we want them to go. We can still have joy even in the mist of living in this difficult world.

My spiritual sister, Carolyn, has been having a hard time in life. The devil has really been on her trail, but through it all Carolyn still has joy. She suffers from real bad seizures and she's constantly seeking God's face for deliverance. One thing I love about Sister Carolyn is that no matter what she is going through, she knows that God still has a purpose and a plan for her life. Hang in there Sister Carolyn. The best is yet to come.

Satan wants to steal our joy, but it's up to us to give it to him. I have learned over the years that if God is for me it really doesn't matter who is against me because the God I serve is more than enough. We can expect the best when it comes from God. God wants us to come real just like little children. Children will say just what's on their mind. When you are real you can love yourself better.

When you are real you don't have to dress like a man when you know you are a woman. When you are real you don't have to dress like a woman when you know God made you a man. Real people are happy people. It's when you try to be somebody else is when you become fake. It's time to stop faking it till you make it and just be real.

PENELOPE "PENNIE" TAYLOR

Chapter 5

YOU ARE SPECIAL TO GOD

Each of us has different life experiences. You may have not come from a nurturing loving family, but through the magnificent power of Jesus Christ you can sense that you are fearfully and wonderfully made by God for a unique and special purpose. Why? Because the Lord says so. To everyone that reads this book know that you are special to God and He has His eyes on you. God longs to have a relationship with us. When you have a relationship with God and a true understanding that without God I am nothing, but with Him, Glory to God I can be everything He has ordained me to be.

No matter what you have done in your life you are still special to God. Stop beating yourself up about what others are saying about you. Stop letting people label you as not being good enough. Stop letting people whisper lies in your ears. Start listening to what God has to say about you.

We must teach our children at an early age that God is in control of their life as well. There is a generation that is coming up after us. It is imperative that we teach them the things of God at an early age.

I thank God that he has given me an ear to hear Him when He speaks to me. If we listen to God he will keep us out of a lot of trouble. I thank God for giving me discernment to know the difference between right and wrong. In the body of Christ God needs people that can discern so that other people can be delivered. If you can discern you can help people get delivered.

A lady once told me that she was mad in church because everybody was shouting and praising God and nobody could tell that she was hurting and going through. We in the body of Christ should be able to look at a person and see that something is not right with them. That's called discernment. Are you a discerning Parent? Are you a discerning friend? Are you really concerned about what others are going through with, or are you really just concerned about yourself?

When we are going through the storms of life all we need to remember is the one that calms the storm and His name is Jesus. Know that prayer changes things. God allows certain things to go wrong in our lives in order to test our faith. I know we hate having our faith tested, because that is when we find out what we are really made of. Having faith means that even though you don't see His hand working in your situation you still believe that He is there for you in the bad times as well as in the good times. You can always find Joy in Jesus no matter what is happening in your life.

Nehemiah 8:10
[10] Then he said unto them, Go your way, eat the fat, and drink the sweet, and send portions unto them for whom nothing is prepared: for this day is holy unto our LORD: neither be ye sorry; for the joy of the LORD is your strength.

We don't have to be sad when we know that the Lord is our strength. We can always find Joy in our risen Savior.

He will be there when there is no one else there. That's what it means to count it all Joy. We don't have to come unglued during out times of testing. God is always working things for our good. We have a God that can always be trusted. We need to P.U.S.H. Pray Until Something Happens. It may not happen overnight or next year, but keep on pushing anyway. I know in due season God will deliver. God's timing always works. God will strengthen you to stand against the enemy.

We need to surround ourselves with people who make us feel like we matter. Surround yourself with people who have your best interest to heart. Surround yourself with people that can help you get to your destiny. Everybody that smiles in your face is not for you. I found out that smiling faces tell lies sometimes.

Jesus said His own familiar friends betrayed Him. So what makes us so special? It's time we learn how to get over some things and move on. If you want your spiritual groove back you have got to learn how to move on.

My heart is heavy for this lost and dying world that doesn't know Jesus in the pardon of their sin. When I was preparing to write my initial sermon, God woke me up and said ENOUGH is ENOUGH! He said to me... I am tired of the lying, I am tired of the gossiping, and I am tired of the backbiting. He said ENOUGH is ENOUGH! I preached that Message on July 27, 2013.

I know that God was well pleased with the assignment that He had given me. When we yield to what God wants us to do there is nothing He will withhold from us.

Psalms 84:11For the LORD God is a sun and shield: the LORD will give grace and glory: no good thing will he withhold from them that walk uprightly.

Just look at all the scriptures in God's word that He has given us to live a wonderful prosperous life. The word will work in our life if we believe that God will do what He says He will do. God will never lie about His word. He has given us 66 books to feast upon. We must find time every day to study God's word. That's the only way we will ever have peace in our life.

Alcohol and drugs might give you joy and peace for a while, but as soon as the drugs wear off all your peace and your joy is gone. Real joy comes from the Lord. I want to keep my joy. Anytime we let people take our joy away from us they are controlling us. When I thought about that, I had to practice daily not to let people steal my joy away from me. It is so easy for Satan to use people to try and steal your joy. He is always roaming around looking for a place to live, but I refuse to let him live inside of me.

We as Christians must always stay connected to God by staying in His word. This Christian race is not about us, it's about God. Somebody reading this book may have reached your turning point in life, but I declare and decree that God will give you your spiritual groove back. It's time to be resurrected in Christ. He came to set the captive free.

The devil has all kinds of tricks to keep you from getting your spiritual groove back so that you can abort your destiny and your purpose. God is with you even in your valley experience. Life may have seemed like it's passing you by, but know that God is a keeper. He will keep you when you need to be kept. He will rock you in the midnight hour. He will dry your tears when nobody else sees you crying. I found this out from an old Deacon by the name of Joseph Rogers. He would always tell me that God is better than good. The more I tried God, I found out for myself that He was and still is better than good.

When you are going through a trial, ride it out. It's all for God's glory. Know that you have the victory in Jesus. He's crazy about you. When He made man He had you in mind. Know that you are special to God.

PENELOPE "PENNIE" TAYLOR

Chapter 6

SPEAK UP

This is a message I preached back in February of 2014. Sometimes in life we don't speak up when we need to speak up, especially in the body of Christ.

Ecclesiastes 3:7A time to rend, and a time to sew; a time to keep silence, and a time to speak;
There will always be times when we need to speak up or simply put, JUST SHUT OUR MOUTH! I've always been a person to speak up and speak out. How many of you know you will be hated by others when you speak up and speak out? Why? Because some people will not like what you have to say.

As children of God we don't always speak up because we are afraid of what someone might think of us if we tell the truth about a situation. We need to speak up for what's right, and we need to speak up for what's wrong. The reason why our churches are in the shape they are in is because nobody wants to speak up. King Solomon tells us in the word of God there's a time to speak up. God wants us to make right choices, which includes speaking up for what is right. God has planned a time for everything under the sun. Our choices should reflect what we value.

Have you heard Christians say just pray about it? That lets you know right then they rather not speak up. Sometimes we have got to do more than pray about a situation. Sometimes you have got to show some action. Action is what faith is all about. When you speak up God has just answered your prayer.

If you read Genesis chapter 18 you will find where Abraham was brave enough to speak to the Lord about destroying the city of Sodom and Gomorrah. If the leaders in the churches would speak up Deacons wouldn't be doing some of the things they are doing. If the leaders would speak up the congregation wouldn't be doing the things they are doing. It parents would speak up our children wouldn't be doing some of the things they are doing. Readers its time we speak up and stand for Jesus. Job chapter 7 verse 11 Job said he will not be quiet. He will speak up in the suffering of his spirit. He said he will complain because He was so unhappy. How many are willing to speak up in the church when you are unhappy?

If Christians would speak up we wouldn't have so many church hoppers. Sometimes other people will not speak up, but they want you to speak up on their behalf. God is looking for someone that will stand for truth in all situations. People are not getting delivered because nobody wants to speak the truth to them anymore. I learned that if you speak the truth God will fight your battles. When a friend says to me, Pennie just tell me the truth, I respond by saying, "If you don't want to know the truth please don't ask me, because I am going to give you the truth." It's time to stop telling people what they want to hear and start telling them what they need to hear.

People are on their way to hell because nobody told them the truth. People don't want you to tell them that same sex marriage is an abomination to God. People don't want you to tell them that you don't need to be shacking up and preaching the gospel. People don't want you telling them that your little girl is going with another little girl or that your little boy just kissed another little boy in the mouth.

It's time to speak up. God does not want us compromising when it comes to speaking up. We as Christians can stop a lot of stuff in our churches, in our communities, in our schools, if we would just speak up. The plan for our life has already been laid out in the word of God. It's time to speak up.

PENELOPE "PENNIE" TAYLOR

Chapter 7

GOD FAVORED ME

My first book I wrote was entitled "TRUST GOD NO MATTER WHAT'. We have got to learn how to trust God no matter what. In my lifetime there are a lot of things I have prayed asking God for. Some He has answered and some He has not answered, but I do know He will answer in HIS OWN TIME AND NOT MINE. If you are frustrated with how your life is going right now, know that we serve a God who is sovereign and who is always there no matter what you do, whether good or bad.

My son Tygel is 36 years old. He has been through a lot of ups and down in his lifetime as we all have. He is a good son. He has never disrespected me or his father, but somewhere along the way he has made a lot of bad choices like we all have. What we decided was that we needed to give our son back to the Lord and let Him work out his situation. We have prayed many years asking God to make a change in our son life. I realize that God has a time for everything and His time is not like our time. Today our son is doing much better than he was yesterday, and we praise God for that.

Sometimes we've got to praise God for the little things as well as the big things that He does for us. Sometimes the Lord will allow our children to go through things just to see how we are going to act. Are we going to curse God and die? When we don't act like the devil wants us to act, that's when God will change the situation around.

Sometimes you've got to confuse the devil. One way we can confuse the devil is to give God some praise when all hell is breaking out in your life. Know that it is only a test. This life we live is only a test. I am so glad that God holds the key to my life. I would not want to serve any other God. We must live by the power of God. That's why I can say Pennie got her groove back, because God stepped in and did a new thing in my life. He stepped in and made me a new person. He stepped in and gave me my Joy back. I know we serve a mighty God who can do anything He wants to do.

Philippians 2:13 For it is God which worketh in you both to will and to do of his good pleasure.

If you want to live a life that pleases GOD THE CHOICE IS UP TO YOU. All we have to do is take one day at a time. Tomorrow will take care of itself.

I love praising my God. He has done more for me than I even thought about doing for myself. On one June morning in 2013 my family and I were traveling to Charlotte N.C. The Queen city. I was so excited about what God has been doing in our lives until I told my husband that I felt like jumping out of the car on the interstate and hollering to everybody how Good God is to us. Prozac or Zoloft can't compare to how good God makes you feel. I have been on Zoloft before, and some of you have to, but the difference is that you don't want anybody to know about it. Sometimes we can't come out of our situation because we want people to think we got it all together. We are looking good on the outside but deep down on the inside we are dead man bones crying out, "Can these bones live?"

I have suffered from seasonal depression since I was in the seventh grade. At the time I didn't know what was wrong with me and my mother didn't either. I would go into deep sleeps and the only thing that would wake me up was my mother's prayers. My mother use to pray for me day and night, hours at the time. She is 91 years old and she is still praying. I love you momma. I use to close my eyes and tell my nieces good bye because I didn't think I would see them again. My mother use to tell me... Baby, don't say that. Everything is going to be alright. I missed weeks out of school because of my condition.

I am now 55 years old, so I know that God had a plan for my life. I learned how to pray from listening to my mother's prayers that she prayed for me when I was sick. About 3 years ago I went to see a doctor and she took my blood work and found out that my vitamin D level was the lowest she had ever seen. She put me on Zoloft and vitamin D to build my count up. It has been two years since I suffered from depression. I thank God for putting Dr. Pauline Bellecci in my path to bring healing to my body.

I know that God works through medicine and I knew that one day I would not have to suffer with seasonal depression. Some of you that feel like you are depressed during winter months from a lack of sunlight like I was, please visit a doctor. You don't have to go for years like I did feeling that way and not knowing what is going on with your body like I did. Now I visit my doctor about every 4 months to make sure my body is in proper working order. We need to begin to count our blessings and not our problems. God always has a plan and I thank Him for favoring me.

PENELOPE "PENNIE" TAYLOR

Chapter 8

NEW BEGINNINGS

Eight is the number of New Beginnings. Do you long for a new start in life? Do you long to see the manifestation of the Lord come alive in your life? Well I am here to tell you God is still in the blessing business. He is looking for people that will obey Him. All you have to do is call on the name of Jesus and He will show you great and mighty things. He has shown me great and mighty things that I did not know about that are finally coming to pass. If I had ten thousand tongues they would not be enough to praise God with. Why? Because He has been so very good to me.

When I look back over the last 55 years of my life I could have been dead and resting in my grave, BUT GOD saw fit for me to live. I know some of you have a BUT GOD situation. It was nobody BUT GOD that saw fit for me to live. Look at what His word says:

Jeremiah 1:5 Before I formed you in the womb I knew you; and before you came forth out of the womb I sanctified you, and I ordained you a prophet unto the nations.
This is what God said to Jeremiah, and He is saying the same thing to us. He has ordained each of us for purpose. It does not matter how old you are, God wants to give you your spiritual groove back. Sometimes it will cost you to get your groove back. We are bought with a price. Jesus paid it all. He wants us to be free to worship Him, free to lift holy hands, free to praise His holy name. I do not serve a dead God.

When I was in the world going to the club hanging out at all times of the night I thought I was having fun, which I was, because I didn't know Jesus. Well I knew of Him but I didn't have a personal relationship with Him like I thought I did. It takes having a relationship with God to stay on this Christian journey. If you don't know God for yourself you are in bad trouble. I bless God on today because He is my all in all. God is my everything. The devil will always try to keep us off track if we let him. We must learn how to deal with the devil on our level before we can go to another level. The devil wants to seal our lips with Polygrip, but I refuse to give in to his tricks. It doesn't matter how many degrees you have you still need Jesus. You can have more degrees than a thermometer you still need Jesus. When you put God first everything else will fall in line.

God is ready to give you a new beginning in this life. He wants you to have the best in this life. He wants you to have peace and joy in this life. People of God are not living up to their calling. God said to me it's time for the body of Christ to tap into the spirit. It's time for us to get along with each other in the house of God. There is a dysfunction in the church that God almighty is not pleased with. When we go through storms in life they don't affect God, they affect us. Whatever you are going through with know that it is only temporary. God is responsible for all your needs. God has you on hold. You just don't have it yet. Delayed does not means denial. If you can hear from God you can make it from where you are to where He wants to take you. Stop listening to the wrong people. Stop listening to the naysayers. If God has spoken to you then you do not need confirmation from people. God didn't bless me my chance, He meant to bless me.

Some of you that are reading this book you have prayed and asked God to do a new thing in your life but you have not seen the promise come alive. God said keep holding on because the best is yet to come. God is trying to teach you something while you are still waiting on Him to move. God said that His timing is not like our timing. His timing is always better than ours. God said when He moves you will know it was nobody but Him. When He brings you out you will know it was nobody but Him. God wants you to have your joy back. He wants you to be alive again. He wants you to feel like you felt when you first receive Him. You don't have to keep living in the past. God wants to give you a new beginning at life.

Pray this prayer:

> Lord, I come to you in the name of Jesus. Lord, I know I have focused on my past, but right now I ask that you take my pass and throw it in the sea of forgetfulness and remember it no more. Lord, I know you will make me over again. Lord, make me new again like only you can do. In Jesus name I pray. Amen

Now get ready for your New Beginning.

PENELOPE "PENNIE" TAYLOR

Chapter 9

ENOUGH IS ENOUGH

Are you sick and tired of being sick and tired? Well if you are this chapter is for you.

I know this lady that God delivered from drugs. 911 means you have an emergency crisis. You are in need of help. Whether you need the ambulance, the police, or the fire department you have an emergency.

If you need a spiritual 911 who would you call? Most people want to call their friend or someone that's close to them. Your mother, your father, your Pastor, your brother or your sister. What if none of them answers your call then what? Have you ever tried calling on Jesus in your emergency crisis?

There's urgency like never before. There's a cry in the spirit realm. What can we do every day to help win someone to Christ? The body of Christ needs to wake up. We have been sleeping too long. God told me enough is enough. Preachers don't want to preach the truth anymore. They don't want to talk about sin, about fornication, about adultery, about repenting, but God let me know enough Is enough. It's time to come clean with God for He already knows our hearts. God is tired of people coming to church and leaving the same way they came. He came to set the captive free. Whom the Son set free is free indeed.

You can believe that truth because that is the living word of God. Jesus is looking for people that will obey His word and stop compromising with the devil. Nowadays you can't tell the saved from the unsaved. God is looking for people that will practice what they preach and stop hiding behind closed doors doing things you shouldn't be doing. If you have any kind of God's spirit in you I do believe you can't live any kind of way you want to because God's word will convict you. The Holy Ghost is a teacher and a keeper if you want to be taught and kept. The Holy Ghost will keep us when we don't think we can keep our self. We try to pour into others, but sometimes we just need God to pour into us. Enough is enough.

Jesus is coming back sooner than we think. It's time for God's people to come together and do what he has called us to do as the body of believers. God is ready to break yokes in your life. In order for you to do what God wants you to do, you must get the yokes broken off of you. If you are sick and tired of being sick and tired it's time to do something about it. It's time out from playing hide and seek.

Are you living in God's perfect will or His permissive will? It's time for a shift in your life. It's time to shift into a new life. It's your season to be all that God has purpose for you to be. If it means giving up some friends that's what you might have to do in order to be about our fathers business. You need to get delivered before you can help somebody else get delivered. If sin is holding you back, repent and get back on track so God can use you. We have the victory in Jesus. I don't know about you, but it took the Holy Ghost to knock the devil out of me. It took the Holy Ghost to knock lying out of me. It took the Holy

Ghost to knock all evil doing out of me. I got to the point where I had to say enough is enough. Jesus let me know I could lean on Him. If you lean on Jesus He won't let you fall. Readers, God has not given us a spirit of fear, but of power, and love and a sound mind. We can trust God.

I was talking to a lady who let me know that her life was not going well. She said she was not happy about where her life was headed. I told her first of all she needs to trust that God is who He says He is and then turn her situation over to Him. The reason why a lot of people are going through hard times is because we want to try and fix the problem instead of giving it to the Lord. I preached a message, "Whose Baggage Are You Carrying?" Sometimes we try to carry our baggage and everybody else's baggage, but I heard God say to me one day, "Enough is enough." Stop letting other people dump their baggage off on you and you stop dumping your baggage off on other people. We've all got some baggage whether we want to deal with it or not.

Solomon says in Ecclesiastes 3:6 There is a time to cast away. We need to let it go. Some things are worthy of treasuring for the rest of our lives, while other things belong in the trash.

Right now I need to clean out my closet. Some things I need to give away and some things I need to throw away. What about all of you? Sometimes in life we need to down size. We need to DE-clutter some things from our life, from our mind, and from our spirit. If you are tired of being stuck in the same spot that you have been in for the last 10 years, it's time to get up and decide from this day forward you have had enough.

Maybe you are angry or bitter with someone you feel has wronged you. Maybe you refuse to forgive the person who told you a lie. Maybe you are having trouble on your job or in your families that we are trying to fix on our own. It's time to let go of the past. I know I have experienced this myself. LETTING GO OF THE PAST.

You cannot get your groove back as long as you keep holding on to the baggage. God did not intend for us to carry the baggage. He wants it all. Will you give it to Him today? Enough is enough.

Chapter 10

SAVE THE LAST DANCE

When I was a young girl I use to love to dance. One reason I didn't want to get saved is because I thought I would have to give up my dancing. Well I didn't give up my dancing after I got saved I just changed partners. After dancing with the devil for so long I decided it was time I start dancing with the Lord.

I gave my life to the Lord on June 25, 1994. I will never forget that night. I went to church with my mother and I just knew I was going to be there half of the night. If you are in Holiness you know what I'm talking about. I went about 8:00pm because you know how some of us like to get there late. Well I was there until 1:00 in the morning calling on the name of Jesus. I tell you the night I got saved was the best night of my life, just to know I didn't have to die and go to hell if I hold out to the end. We must endure the race if we want to see Jesus. I found out Jesus is the best thing that has ever happened to me. I love dancing before the Lord. I found out that He is more than enough. I found out that He is my great provider when my money starts acting funny. I found Him to be my friend in the midnight hour when all my other friends are asleep.

We have so many things going on in our world today. Suicide is a big stronghold right now. My prayer is for everyone that is going through a dark time in your life, I want you to know that you can find your way back to God.

49

Repeat this prayer after me...

> Father God in the name of Jesus, Lord, I
> love you. Lord, I honor your holy name.
> Lord, I am in a dark place right now and I
> ask that you come into my heart right now
> and anything that is not of you, I ask that
> you remove it and make me clean again.
> Lord, I don't want to take my life and I need
> you to step in and rescue me right now in
> the name of Jesus I pray. Amen.

If you really believe this prayer I know that Jesus will
restore you back to your place in God.

My mission is to bring souls into the kingdom of God. My
mission is to help a lost soul find their way back to God,
whether man woman, boy, or girl we all need Jesus in our
life.

It's so easy to get off track, but we have someone that is
standing in the gap for us and His name is Jesus. He is
making intercessions with His father on our behalf. I thank
God that I can dance, dance, dance and I am nowhere near
tired. Why? Because the Joy of the Lord is my strength.

I know sometimes the road seems like it's too hard to
walk, but if we depend on God He will get us to our place
on time. God has given each one of us a purpose in this
life. Seek God for your purpose. When God gives you a
purpose you can't be listening to other people, because if
you do you just might miss your purpose.

People love to tell you what you need to do and what you

should be doing, but they don't have all the answers. God saved us for a purpose. In the book of Genesis Joseph was criticized because he had a dream. Do you have a dream? Don't let the enemy stop you from dreaming. Did you stop your purpose because you were criticized? Did you stop going forward because somebody put your name out in the streets? Did you stop going to church because somebody talked about you? Out of every family God will use you for a purpose. Family members will get mad when God begins to elevate you. Friends will walk away when God begins to bless you with more. Don't let what people say about you cause you to turn away from God. One thing the devil doesn't like is when we laugh in his face. Tell that devil you are more than a conquer through Christ Jesus. Tell him you are the head and not the tail. Tell him that no weapon formed against you shall prosper.

It's time to get your groove back and start dancing with the Lord again. Don't let people stop you from dancing with the Lord. I use to like dancing with the stars, but now I can dance with Jesus. What a great day it will be when I meet my Savior face to face and I hear Him say. I saved the last dance just for you.

PENELOPE "PENNIE" TAYLOR

Chapter 11

CAN I GET A R-E-F-I-L-L?

I'm talking about how to get your groove back. Like I said earlier, I thank God that I got my spiritual groove back. So many people are giving up on God because they feel like they don't have a way out of their situation, but baby I am here to tell you God is better than anyone that is against you. Sometimes we got to get from around some people so these dry bones can live. You might feel like you have reached your turning point, but keep pressing forward in the Lord. This Christian race is not about us, it's about the Lord. I get so much Joy when I think about all the wonderful things the Lord has done for me and my family. We have the victory In Jesus. It took the Holy Ghost to knock the devil out of me and I thank God for His anointing Holy Ghost Power. I heard Jesus say I can lean on Him.

This is your season for favor. This is your season for breakthrough. This is your season for greatness. Whatever you are believing God for, know that He can be trusted. Trust God like never before. When the odds are against you continue to trust God. When your family and friends walk away trust God. Even in the mist of your downs look up. Jesus is up not down. Stop tripping. God's not finish with you yet. You may be in a storm right now but there is light at the end of the tunnel. A just man falls seven times but guess what? He gets back up again. So no matter how many times you fall you can still get back up again. So when you fall, know that you don't have to stay down. God is more than enough. We all go through a season of drought, but during those seasons, God is molding us and shaping us into the men and women of God that He want us to be. You don't have to waddle in self-pity. You don't have to stay in defeat. If you can change your thinking you can change your situation. If we seek God for counsel He will take care of all our needs. If you need a refill look at Acts chapter 2.

1 And when the day of <u>Pentecost</u> was fully come, they were all with one accord in one place.
2 And suddenly there came a sound from <u>heaven</u> as of a rushing mighty wind, and it filled all the house where they were <u>sitting</u>.
3 And there appeared unto them cloven tongues like as of fire, and it sat upon each of them.
4 And they were all filled with the Holy <u>Ghost</u>, and began to speak with other tongues, as the <u>Spirit</u> gave them utterance.

If you need to be filled ask God. Once God fills you your life will never be the same. Sometimes we run on empty but Jesus is our filling station. The word of God is our filling station. Just like we need to have our cars service we also need to have our spiritual body service through the word of God.

When God fills you He deposits something on the inside of you that feels like fire shut up in your bones. My prayer is that God doesn't take His spirit from me. It's His spirit that makes me talk right. It's His spirit that makes me hold my tongue when my flesh wants me to cuss somebody out. It's His spirit that makes me love people that I know are unlovable. I thank God for depositing so much inside of me. I thank God because now I can tell somebody else how to get there groove back. Imagine what can happen in our churches when the people of God get on one accord. We are fighting over who gone get the offering next Sunday. We are fighting over who gone lead the songs in the choir. People of God it's time we be about our fathers business and come together as one as God would desire us to be. Together we stand and united we fall. We need a great awakening in our cities, in our churches, in our schools and in our homes. It's time we seek God like never before. God is coming sooner than we think. My question to you is. Is your house in order?

God has already told us in His word that in the last days He was going to pour out His spirit among all flesh. I want to be in position to receive all that God has for me. We must keep our hearts and minds focused on the Lord. Every day the enemy tries to bring stuff to tare the people of God down. We don't have to listen to the lies of the enemy any longer. Jesus has come to set the captive free and when He sets us free we are free indeed.

God is a healer and He's making a way for you and for me. He wants to fill you with his Holy Spirit. When you get a refill you will learn how to treat your neighbor right and the people that you come in contact with every day. When you get a refill the Holy Spirit will guide and direct you when to speak and when to shut up. I thank God for shutting my mouth when it needs to be shut.

I tell you God's anointing is awesome. You can't have God's anointing and live any kind of way. God is always there. If you make your bed in hell God is there. The Holy Spirit can come on you anywhere: In I.C.U; on your sick bed; on your job; at your school; in your car; wherever you may be God can meet you there.

I thank God for His anointing that is on my life. I realize I am bought with a price and that price is Jesus. It's time to get rid of our heavy load, because Jesus is a HEAVY LOAD BEARER. Whatever is holding you back from God's best you need to get rid of it and let it go? God will give you a double portion for all you have been through. He will give you a double portion of whatever you need to get your spiritual groove back. He will give you beauty for your ashes.

All you have to do is be sincere and
ask God for a R-E-F-I-L-L.

Chapter 12

JOURNEY AMONG SISTERS

I preached this message in Irmo, South Carolina on September 27th 2014. I tell you God really did bless the sisters that were in attendance. When God shows up He shows out. I prayed and asked God to use me like never before and He did just that. God knew who was going to be there and He knew what each lady needed. I always pray and ask God to give me discernment whenever I have to speak, because women are hurting and we as ministers need to know how to discern someone's pain.

Are you your sister's keeper? Are you a real sister? Now we've got all kinds of sisters. We've got sneaky sisters. We've got jealous sisters. We've got gossiping sisters. We've got envious sisters, just to name a few. What kind of sister are you? We've still got some sisters that have your back in the good times as well as in the bad times, but are you on a journey with your sisters?

God has called us to love our sister as ourselves. Do you just love your sister when she's doing everything you want her to do for you? Do you love your sister when she's scandalizing your name and calling you everything except a child of God? I want you to know everybody that smiles in your face is not for you. Don't be fooled by a kiss. Everybody is not out to get you but some are. God will reveal the snakes to you. All snakes don't crawl on their belly. Some walk on two feet.
Some people you will have to leave behind in this next

season. All your sisters can't go on the journey with you. I want you to know that sometimes the journey will get hard. Sometimes the journey will get weary and make you want to give up and throw in the towel. Sometimes on the journey you are going to get your feelings hurt. People are going to talk about you on the journey. Sometimes on the journey you are not going to get your way. Sometimes on the journey you will have to do some things you don't want to do and go places you don't want to go, but if God called you to it, He was take you through it. You've got to learn how to take a licking and keep on ticking.

On this journey you've got to learn not to carry your feelings on your shoulder. No matter what goes on in your life you've got to stay on the journey. Don't give up, and don't give in. This is not the time to sit on the side of the bed crying about your problems. I want you to know that God feels your pain and He knows all about your troubles. God is able to do all that we ask or think, because He is just that kind of God. God is about to bring your child out the crack house. God is able to take away your addiction no matter what it is. God is able to fulfill your needs in time of crisis. If we ask anything in Jesus name He will do. That's what the word says.

Four teenagers at my church asked us to pray for them to get a job and guess what? All four of them are working now and they are paying their tithes. They are praising God for what He is doing for them. God's grace is amazing.

I wouldn't want to live without God's amazing Grace. Ladies it's time we be about God's business. It's time to stop being jealous and envious of one another. It's time to stop carrying on because of what somebody did to you five years ago. What God has done for others He will do the same for you if you would only trust and believe?

I know some times you single women feel burned out because you have to carry the load by yourself, but I found God to be a heavy load bearer. He will always be there whenever you need Him. Sometimes He might not answer when you call Him but He will be there right on time. It's time to get your spiritual groove back and the only way to do that is to get connected to God.

PENELOPE "PENNIE" TAYLOR

Chapter 13

HOW MOMMA GOT OVER

I want to dedicate this last chapter in memory of my mother. My momma was born on February 14, 1923 which is Valentine's Day, a day fit for a queen. My mother passed away on April 6, 2015 at the beautiful age of 92. My mother was a praying woman. She was the only lady I knew that would fast from eating food for three and a half days and she did that for over sixty years and didn't lose weight because she was feed on the word of God. My mother said if she didn't fast she wouldn't last and she was very serious about that. My mother knew that the joy of the Lord was her strength. My mother raised my siblings and me in the projects in a single family home, but I think we all turned out pretty good. I was always reminded, it's not where you come from but where you are going. My mother raised her children up in church. The word of God says in Proverbs 22:6 Train up a child in the way he should go: and when he is old, he will not depart from it.

I tell you, your children may stray but they will come back. I'm still believing God for some of my family members to come back and I know they will. I was one of them Drug babies. I was drug to church. I was drug to Sunday school. I was drug to B.T.U. What we called in my growing up days which stands for Baptist Training Union. We had to go every Sunday evening. Nowadays you do good to get Christians to go to church twice a month. I thank God my mother gave me the foundation at an early age. I use to say when I grow up I am never going to church, but where am I now? In Church. Why? Because it was instilled in me at an early age. We can't wait until our children are teenagers and then decide we are going to try and raise them because it will be to late then. The bible says if we spare the rod we will spoil the child. Them children need their behind whipped when they are small.

We've got children now days who don't give anybody respect and don't even have respect for themselves. What happen to parents being the head of the home? It's time for the parents to take the authority back in their homes and over their children that God gave them... God is going to hold parents accountable for what we let our children do when they were entrusted to our care. Once they are grown they are responsible for themselves. As long as we continue to baby our kids they will never grow up to be responsible adults. My momma whipped my behind almost every week, but now I thank her because I could have been on the chain gang which we call prison in this generation.

Children these days think you owe then something. They are so lazy and disrespectful. It's time we teach our sons and daughters how to live holy and how to live godly lives. Children pick up what they see and hear, and you wonder why your child went to school and cussed the teacher out, because they heard you're cussing somebody out and we thank its cute. There were certain words we were not allowed to say in my mother's house.

My mother was a woman that practiced what she preached. She was a Sunday school teacher at the age of ninety one; she was the president of the home mission at the age of ninety one. She was nice and kind to everyone she meet. She was a dignified woman. She would always let people take advantage of her and treat her any kind of way. One day I told my mother to let me tell them off for her because I wasn't saved. My mother told me to keep my mouth shut and let God handle them. My momma was always right. I would watch to see if God was going to handle them and he did.

My mother was a praying woman as I said early. I remember one time my mother told me not to go to the club but my fast self decided I was going to go anyway. Well my mother was asleep and I thought I could sneak out the house before she woke up. When she woke up and I was not home she came and got me out of the club and brought my fast self back home. Anything could have happened to me for being disobedient.

I never knew we were poor until I grew up and my childhood friends say we were some of the best-dressed children in the projects. We might not have had everything we wanted, but we sure did have everything we needed and most of all we had God in our home. Whether we wanted to go to church or not we were going, and if we didn't go we had to be sick or about dead. Our punishment was that we were not going outside and play for the rest of the day. I tell you what, we got to feeling better real quick.

Two days after my mother's 92nd birthday she had a heart attack and she stayed in the hospital for a week before moving her to the nursing home. She stayed in the nursing home for about two months before her death. She was tired of suffering and I knew she was ready to meet the Lord. I had traveled to Texas for my daughter's graduation even though I knew how sick my mother was. I asked God not to take my mother until I got back.

Now the word of God says to make your request known, so I put God to the test and did just that. God allowed me to come back home and two weeks later he took my mother. The night before my mother passed I told God whenever he was ready to take my mother just let her go in peace without any pain. How many of you all know we serve an awesome God because the next day after the nurse gave my mother a bath her heart just stopped beating. I thank God because everything I asked Him to do He did it.

If you walk upright before God he will withhold nothing from His children. I thank God that I know how to call on him for myself. My mother taught me how to pray because I watched her pray. She would pray for hours at a time. I could sneak off somewhere because I knew that when I got back she would never know I was gone because she would still be on her knees. That's the kind of praying momma I had.

Readers it's not too late to call on the name of Jesus. Whatever you are believing God to do for you just ask him. If it is in His will he will grant it to you. My mother has prayed for so many people while on her Christian journey that some knew about it and some didn't. My mother prayed for all of the children in Bailey Heights because she knew how bad we were. Some of us made it through because Mother Blackshear prayed for us. I want to know there is always somebody praying for me and my family. We need prayer in our life to make it on this Christian journey. I want my readers to know that momma got over through fasting and praying and so can you.

Rest in Peace
Momma
Your Baby Girl,
Pennie

TESTIMONIES

WE GOT OUR GROOVE BACK

My Sisters and Brothers' Testimonies

These are the Testimonies of some ladies and men who are not afraid to let the world know what they have been through and what it took for them to overcome it. Read their story because I am sure you have a story of your own to tell. If I could help just one person as I pass through this life then I know that my living is not in vain.

Testimony 1

For some reason, I could not get to sleep due to thinking about the comedian Robin Williams. This man committed suicide due to depression and probably a related illness. He had money, family and friends that loved him... yet, he hung himself. I wonder why he didn't go to somebody and tell them what he was feeling, and tell them this is something he can't handle by himself. He was surrounded by everyone who loved him, yet he felt alone, like he was the only person in the world who is dealing with an illness that was torturing his mind. I am quite sure he tried to get rid of the feeling by doing ungodly jesters, yet that didn't help. I am also sure he wanted to talk about his illness with his family, etc., but he wouldn't because they probably would have told him he is just going through a phase in his life right now and that is the last thing he needed to hear. So, instead of his family, friends and fans thinking he was crazy, he chose to take the only way out that he felt was best for him....suicide.

Unfortunately, that is what so many people do whenever they suffer from MAJOR DEPRESSION, BIPOLAR or any illness dealing with one's mind. If you were to ask a person which illness would they rather have as compared to mental illness (let's name a few: CANCER, AIDS, HERPES, BEING BLIND, MISSING LIMBS... I'll stop there b/c I think everyone has the point), that person would choose to have all that I just listed before they have mental illness. Why? With mental illness, it's dealing with your brain. Your brain is what makes you the person you are. Once mental illness starts controlling it, you are not that same person.

The cells in your brain are totally offset and when that happens. You will start experiencing so many torturous symptoms that you cry out to God to take you out of your misery.

Yes, doctors give you medicine to try to control the illness, if one medicine doesn't work, they try others. In other words, they are experimenting trying to see what will temporally work for you. Man can help with medication, but man has no cure for mental illness, and it can happen to anyone. It does not discriminate from anyone, even if you can be the smartest person on earth.

The reason I am telling you this is, watch your love ones and if you see a change in them, please do not turn your back on them. Just because they look healthy means nothing.

Finally I would like my fb family and friends to know, I have been suffering from this illness since I was 35 years old. Major depression as well as bipolar disorder and yes I am a miracle for being here because GOD brought me back after taking 200 deadly pills. Please keep this in mind I you read what I am about to share with you....

I fell into a deep sleep and woke up in an unfamiliar place. Yes I was afraid because I knew I wasn't alone, but I could not see anyone. I was hot and some BEING started leading me to a hole in which there is no escape. My senses made me realize this BEING was taking me into the PIT OF HELL. Then it came to me about what the BIBLE teaches about suicide. I then started pleading to GOD and asking him to forgive me for killing myself. I remember looking down in a hot hole and hearing people yelling out to GOD to save them. The BEING let go of my arms and I remember crying and asking GOD to save me because I did not belong in that place. I was on my knees crying and looking down when I felt the presence of love overtaking me. I was told not to look up and I didn't, but I knew whoever was standing over me was HOLY and I was safe from that hole. Then I heard the sweetest sound saying, "YOU WILL NOT DIE". I remember waking up in my bed and thought I must have had a bad dream. No it wasn't a bad dream. I was in a part of HELL, but GOD'S LOVE and HIS MERCY brought me back.

This is my first time relating my entire experience to anyone. I knew I would need to when the time was right. HELL is real and if you do not have a personal relationship with JESUS, HELL is where you will spend eternity. Please be real with GOD because he loves you so much. Some people say GOD loves people too much to put them in HELL. No, GOD does not put people in HELL.

He has given us a step by step guide on how we want to live after death. HEAVEN or HELL. Those steps are listed in the book called the BIBLE. GOD gives us that choice, and I pray that you choose HEAVEN because HELL is no place you want to be. Take it from someone who was in a part of HELL. Keep love in your heart. Yes, we are made of flesh and may get out of the WILL of GOD. Ask for forgiveness and do all you can to stay in his WILL.

Before I end this letter, I thank my husband for helping me to cope with my illness. I realize some spouses choose not to go through all the different emotions that this illness may put you through, so besides God, my husband is my hero because only he can tell you all the different emotions an trials he has,(and still does) put up with me.

Through the GRACE of GOD, I am doing so much better than I was in the past. I KEPT THIS TO MYSELF FOR TWO LONG YEARS, BUT I REALIZE I MUST SHARE MY EXPERIENCE BECAUSE SO MANY PEOPLE ARE SUFFERING FROM THIS ILLNESS BUT FEEL THE ONLY WAY OUT IS HARMING THEMSELVES. GOD IS THE ANSWER AND HE WILL BE THERE FOR YOU. ALL HE WANTS US TO DO IS ASK, HAVE THE FAITH AND PUT IT IN HIS HANDS.

IF MY TESTIMONY COULD SAVE ONE LIFE FROM THE ENTRAPMENT OF SATAN, THEN I HAVE DONE THE WILL OF GOD. BE BLESS MY FRIEND.

THIS HAPPENED TO ME ABOUT TWO YEARS AGO AND I WAS TOO ASHAMED TO SHARE IT DUE TO HOW PEOPLE WOULD JUDGE ME. GOD ALLOWED ME TO HAVE THE COURAGE TO TELL MY TESTIMONY, ESPECIALLY AFTER THE DEATH OF ROBIN WILLIAMS. THAT REALLY TUGGED AT MY HEART BECAUSE I PASSED AWAY AS WELL AND EXPERIENCE SOMETHING THAT I WILL NEVER FORGET. I THANK GOD EVERYDAY FOR SAVING ME BECAUSE HE DIDN'T HAVE TO, BUT HE DID.

ONCE AGAIN, PENNIE THANK YOU SO MUCH BECAUSE SO MANY PEOPLE ARE COMMITTING SUICIDE BEHIND THIS HORRIBLE ILLNESS.

I AM PRAYING AND ASKING GOD TO LEAD ME TO WRITE A BOOK CONCERNING MENTAL ILLNESS AND BIPOLAR, EVEN THOUGH THEIR IS MUCH MATERIAL OUT THERE FOR ANYONE TO EDUCATE THEMSELVES ON. NO ONE CAN GENERATE SUCH INFORMATION AS A PERSON WHO

ACTUALLY HAS THE ILLNESS. I PRAY THIS LETTER WOULD HELP SOMEONE WHO MAYBE IN A SIMILAR CRISIS. THANK YOU AND MAY GOD BLESS YOU.

Francis Burse
Waycross, Georgia

Testimony 2

This is my Testimony to the youth and to the teenagers that want to be grown up before your time. My name is Tianna Taylor and I am 15 years old. I am learning from my mistakes and I hope you will too.

The scripture says in Ephesians Chapter 6 verses 1-4.
[1] Children, obey your parents in the Lord: for this is right.
[2] Honor thy father and mother; which is the first commandment with promise;
[3] That it may be well with thee, and thou mayest live long on the earth.
[4] And, ye fathers, provoke not your children to wrath: but bring them up in the nurture and admonition of the Lord.

Exodus 20:12 says,
Honor thy father and thy mother: that thy days may be long upon the land which the LORD thy God giveth thee.

And I want to live a long life, but I know if I am disrespecting my elders it will shorten my days. I thought it was time for me to wake up and seek God to turn my life around and put me back on the right path. I realize I have people that love me and care about me. Thank you Pastor Billy and Minister LaWanda Taylor and all my Walking by Faith church family that prayed for me, and will continue to pray for me.

It is no fun having to report to a probation officer twice a week and get permission to do anything when I could have just ask my grandparents who cared for me. Because of my actions I now have to suffer the consequences. I know that everything happens for a reason and I know that God will see me through anything.

My grandparents have always taken my sister and me to church since day one. They set the foundation for us. Thank you Grandma Pennie, and Grandpa Burnar. Thank you Grandma Shirley and Grandpa Terry for taking us in. I love you all. I thank God I have two loving aunties Jessica and Nyga that will do anything for my sister and me. They help keep us on the right track and they help us in school when our grades begin to slip. I thank my church family because you are always there for me. I know now that my place is in God. I will seek to do what I can while I can for the Lord. I know that if I am obedient, God will give me long life. And I thank you.

Tyanna Taylor
Waycross, Georgia

Testimony 3

On this day January 28, 1 year ago my life changed. I left work headed to class to take my health assessment test for nursing school. Made an 86 on the test. Little did I know that was the last test I would take in nursing?

As I headed home the snow began to fall. My car slid, fish tailed and flipped 5 times, my left leg going thru the roof and landing upside down. I laid out there for about two hours. God touched the heart of one of my class mates Lindsey C. Hall. When she didn't see me behind her, she turned around to find me. They cut me out of my car, loaded me on the back of a pickup truck to take me to the ambulance.

There's so much I don't remember, but I began to lose my appetite and after doing all they could my leg could not be saved. I remember before going into surgery I cried about 15 seconds, saying Lord, let your will be done and they rolled me in.

When I woke up I was on the ventilator, lungs paralyzed with a treach, feeding tube, catheter, bowel tube, and a weak right atrium that couldn't pump blood through my heart and one leg. I went in the hospital Jan 28, 2014 and didn't come out until March 26, 2014. I would tell you of the warfare I was in during my time on the ventilator, but if you aren't spiritual minded you wouldn't believe it.

Death was being pronounced while the Holy Ghost was yet speaking life. The Spirit of God will stand and speak for you when you can't utter a word! I know, I have the treach scar to prove it. Through it all GOD kept me. Death had to take a seat, because God said LIVE!!!

Today I am doing well.

Rodney Hardy
Gordo, Alabama

Testimony 4

I Thank God for Jesus who is the head of all of our lives. If it had not been for the Lord on my side, along with the help of my family and a small, but very supportive group of friends and loved ones, my journey of life lessons would have not been an easy road for me to travel on. MY motto in life is...

> Pain made me better so that God could allow me to live in my greater.

God has a way of getting our attention and it may not feel good, but if you learn from the lessons He brings forth in your life, let them make you better and not bitter. I would be willing to go through the experience all over again if I had to because I know I serve a God that will bring me through anything. My Past and my Present equals I'm in love with my Future. God did it, not man so it's finished.

Shonda Tripp
Waycross,
Georgia

PENELOPE "PENNIE" TAYLOR

Testimony 5

My testimony would be how Satan tried to stop me from receiving my Blessings on the day of Evangelist Helen Moody's women conference. I remembered how my sister, Minister Pennie Taylor, asked me to go but I did not want to. I heard my mother say that I needed to go. I was really depressed at the time because of me being sick. But I know it was nobody but God who gave me second thoughts about going. I went through those obstacles with the train being on the track trying to figure out how to get to the other side so I could find the building because the train had stopped on the tracks for miles, I also got lost. But I finally made it after I stopped at a gas station to see how I could get around that train {NOBODY BUT GOD} and that is when I got my breakthrough. Thank You Lord. People I tell you whenever you hear the Lord speaking to you please listen because he is trying to get a blessing to you.

I thank God for giving me another chance to come back to him. After I came back to the Lord my life has never been the same. I can truly say I got my groove back. I am now in a church serving God and doing his will because I listened to His voice.

Susan Gibbs
Lexington, S.C.

PENELOPE "PENNIE" TAYLOR

THANK YOU

I would like to thank you all for your Testimonies. I know someone will be truly set free and delivered because you were not afraid to tell the world how God brought you through. To my readers I know this book has blessed your spirit as you read from front to back. I hope you felt God's presence as this book has been anointed just for you. If Pennie can get her groove back, so can you.

NOTES FOR YOUR SPIRITUAL JOURNEY

PENELOPE "PENNIE" TAYLOR

ABOUT THE AUTHOR

Minister Penelope "Pennie" Taylor was born and raised in the city of Waycross, Georgia where she resides there. She is a 1978 graduate of Waycross High School in Waycross, Georgia. She is married to her husband of 34 wonderful years Deacon Burnar Taylor, and together they have three children.

She is a dedicated member of Walking by Faith Ministries under the Leadership of Pastor Billy and Minister LaWanda Taylor. She was lincensed to Preach the Gospel on July 27,2013 She doesn't mind preaching what thus says the Lord.

She is the Founder and C.E.O. of Women of Destiny, a Ministry that God birthed out of her on April 20,2013. Her mission is to bring healing to women from all walks of life who are hurting and feel that all hope is gone.

She is a Published Author of "TRUST GOD NO MATTER WHAT" and HOW PENNIE GOT HER GROOVE BACK. As she goes higher in the Lord she expects God to do just what He says HE will do.

(Psalms 34:8) "O taste and see that the Lord is good blessed is the man that trusteth in HIm.

PENELOPE "PENNIE" TAYLOR

CONTACT INFORMATION

Email address:

Brownhoneyrum@aol.com

And the rum is for the Holy Spirit that stirs up in me.

Facebook name:

Pennie Taylor

Mailing address is:

Penelope "Pennie" Taylor

P.O. BX 2344

WAYCROSS, GA 31502

www.ingramcontent.com/pod-product-compliance
Lightning Source LLC
LaVergne TN
LVHW021613080426
835510LV00019B/2555